The Layman
Examines
His Faith

by GUSTAVE A. FERRÉ

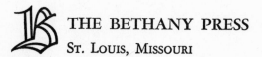

THE BETHANY PRESS
ST. LOUIS, MISSOURI

Library of Congress Catalogue Card Number: 60—7385

1. Christianity -- Essence, genius, nature.

Printed in the United States of America

4576

BR 121.2
.F38
1940

Theology

The Layman Examines His Faith

To

My wife, Dorothy,
and my five children,
Susan, Carl, Loren,
Martha, Elizabeth

Preface

"Of making many books there is no end." This quotation from Ecclesiastes is correct. There can be no end to Christians witnessing to their faith, for each person is under obligation to present what he believes as clearly and as simply as possible. This is my only reason for adding yet another book to the already overabundance of books directed to the layman in the field of the Christian faith.

This book is not written for the scholar or for the trained clergy but rather for the layman. The aim is simply to express clearly and simply what I feel to be central to the Christian faith. My hope and prayer are that every person who reads this book may come to know more and more of the glorious gospel of God's love in Christ.

The ideas and thoughts are only my own as I have accepted them into my own life and thought. Those readers who are acquainted with the writings of my brother, Nels Ferré, will notice that these words are but footnotes on his thought. I am so deeply indebted to him that this brief book could better have been written under joint authorship. Nels is not only a tremendous thinker and consecrated Christian but one who makes the word "brother" beautiful and rich with meaning.

A special word of thanks must be expressed to my family who have been my greatest supporters in urging me to witness to the Christian faith. Words will never be able to express the indebtedness I feel toward them.

GUSTAVE FERRÉ

Contents

9

Contents

Chapter I

The Christian Faith—
Fact or Fantasy

The story is told of an Armenian named Joe. Joe had the finest lamb in all Armenia, with the longest and softest fleece.

The lamb was so famous that Joe's neighbors worried lest it be stolen. One day the robbers came. When Joe saw them coming, he carried the lamb into his cabin and barred the door. He began shooting at the robbers, first from the window on the east, then from the window on the west, then from the east again. But each time he crossed the room, he tripped and fell over the lamb. Finally he opened the door, kicked the lamb outside, and went on fighting.

At times the layman wonders if the church has not been guilty of a similar kind of stupidity. Tripping over its treasured faith and finally exasperated, the church finds that it is simpler to fight without it.

11

We may well ask ourself, "What is the Christian faith?" In effect, it is sinful man transformed by God and freed by his Son from the power of sin; a new man ready to accept God in full trust; old things gone and all things made new.

How true this faith seems when life is full with the presence of God. Yet how false it seems when everything goes wrong. How frustrating to pray and sense nothing real. How futile when our subconscious depths seem to make us cranky, self-accusing, complaining—just plain hard to live with.

Believe all we can, try our hardest, still we are defeated, as though someone else or something else lived our lives. "Old things gone and all things made new" seems to be a lie. Then we have to ask ourselves the question: Is the Christian faith fact or fantasy? Is it the power of God for actual salvation or a man-made device for concealing human folly and weakness?

As in every age, so in this age, life shifts back and forth between hope and despair. Life has its high moments of happiness and its long stretches of wind in the sails, but it has also its depths of despair and the long stretches when the prevailing wind is against us. Some drink its mixture of gladness and gall privately, often in pained silence. Others share it freely with others. Some give up mentally —putting already overcrowded institutions under even greater strain; some drag on mentally—hiding fears and hurts while fearing and hurting others; some take their own physical life, not considering what life ahead may be; others spin in the rut—longing for death but fearful of life to come.

How can man escape this contradiction? One fact is certain: no faith, claiming to be Christian, that paints life or salvation as easy will do. A second fact is even more certain: no faith that lacks a great view of God, one that is relevant to life as it is, will do. Of this we can be sure: the Christian faith is completely realistic.

How can man come to feel that he belongs by nature and destiny to a good God who is all for him and fully able to help him? The biblical faith teaches that man, though he belongs to God by creation, is fearful of God and rebels against him. The biblical faith tells us that man, though God intended he should be good and find happiness, has become spoiled and suffers misery. It balances its insistence on man as the creation of a good God with the recognition that man is actually a sinner who wants his own way—not God's. Emil Brunner quite rightly calls man a creature in contradiction. Though he is made for the goodness of God, he shrinks from it; though he longs for the presence of God, he dares not remain in it; though he defines his destiny in the light of the divine image, he lives his life in the darkness of the enthroned ego.

The term "faith" needs clarification, for it is the most frequently misunderstood of the essential Christian words. It is interpreted in several ways—each with its contribution to the full meaning, each contributing to error when used alone. In its root meaning, faith may denote the following: The Christian religion is based upon facts of which the New Testament is an accurate and trustworthy record. These facts are of the life, death, resurrection, and ascension of Jesus, and the apostolic interpretation of these facts. Faith, thus, consists in believing these facts.

Alexander Campbell stressed this meaning of faith when he wrote:

No testimony, no faith: for faith is only the belief of testimony, or confidence in testimony as true. To believe without testimony is just as impossible as to see without light. The measure, quality, and power of faith are always found in the testimony believed.

Where testimony begins, faith begins; where testimony ends, faith ends.[1]

However, there must be a will to believe if faith is to be produced. Man must be willing to examine the evidence with an open mind, with an honest desire to know; or all the evidence in the world will never evoke faith.

Faith confronts us with the demand for decision. Though we believe because of what God has done, is, and promises, we do the believing. God has shown us him in whom we should believe. He offers us the full assurance of faith. But this assurance requires the trusting heart. True faith unites testimony and trusting in holy wedlock.

I

Full belief and total trust are not enough for Christian faith. It must have the content of biblical faith, for God's gift of the Bible is for the eyes of faith. The Bible is the holy Word of God, the core content for an empty age, which reveals its content only when we accept and understand it aright. It is (1) the way of the world, (2) seen

---

[1] From *The Christian System*, p. 113.

through the mind of Christ, (3) for the power of the Spirit.

(1) When we call the Bible *the way of the world,* we mean, simply, that in it we find the story of human experience in general and of our own humanity in particular. The Bible does not wax romantic or sentimental. It portrays actual life. People sin in it, love in it, lie in it, tell the truth in it, grow corrupt in it, practice social concern in it, fall victim to political intrigue in it, achieve high statesmanship in it. Human hatred has its say in the Bible: a psalmist blesses the practice of dashing the children of one's neighbor against a stone. Human compassion has its say in the Bible: Hosea pulls an unfaithful wife home with cords of love. Works of history make the Bible; so do works of imagination. Modest claims mark the pages of Holy Writ; so do proud boasts. Reliable hopes find their way into the Scriptures; so do fantastic dreams.

The Bible exhibits little selectivity in its portrayal of the ways of the world. It mirrors the evil as well as the good in human nature and experience. The biblical painting of human experience provides an ancient version of realistic art. Whatever may happen to man in the future has already happened to man in the Bible. The Bible introduces us to ourselves. The Bible does not idealize human experience; it illustrates it. It does not debunk human experience; it divulges it. It neither accuses nor excuses human experience; it recalls and relates it. It reveals to man both his terrible misery and his singular grandeur. God gave man the Bible that he might have a looking glass for the soul. Just as our inability to vacate our bodies keeps us from seeing ourselves as we appear to our neighbors, our ambition and pride keep us from seeing ourselves as we appear to God. Just as we need a physical mirror to see our faces as they are, we need a moral and spiritual mirror to see our hearts as they are. The Bible is this mirror.

The biblical mirror reveals us to ourselves in the light of God. Indeed, only this divine illumination keeps it from being just another mirror. God's light enables us to see ourselves not only truly but fully, not only as we actually are but as we ought to be, not only as the servant of sin but as the slave of Christ, not only as the self by which men know us but as the self for which God made us. This mirror does the signal service of revealing to us the God-man. Biblical faith does not become Christian faith unless and until in the Bible we meet Christ. The Bible leads us to a true understanding of ourselves, of our nature and history, only as it brings us to look at them against the portrait of man drawn by God. God became man to show us himself, to show us ourselves, and to remake us after the image of his Son. Without the Bible we could not see ourselves as we are since only the Bible mirrors us against the stature of God's intention for us.

What we see in the Bible depends in some measure on what we are. The farther we stand from the mind of Christ, the less we see it in the Bible—and the less we want to see it in ourselves. The nearer we approach the mind of Christ, the more we see it in the Bible—and the more we want to see it in ourselves. In the Bible we behold every shade of darkness and light. Despite its definite meaning, the Bible confuses those of us who divorce vision from action, who separate study and discipleship. We find in it neither truth nor obedience. The biblical Word cannot penetrate the spiritual blindness of the unbeliever. His unbelief blinds him both to his true self and his actual self. He sees only a dim reflection of himself in the mirror of the Word. Unbelief chooses dim shadows rather than the true image.

(2) *The mind of Christ* is the love of God. God is the personal Spirit who is holy love. Christ is the commanding Presence of the mirror. In his face we see the glory of God and the hope of man. We see an unfailing love without limit of place, personality, or time. We meet holy love in a person who addresses us, who shows us what we are, and who calls us to what we should become.

In Christ we meet both the love that invites and the love that qualifies the invitation with a firm insistence on our fulfillment of certain conditions. In the Bible we see the eternal God, the Father of all creatures, offering himself to us and for us as companion and friend. The Father comes not as the utterly different but as one of us. He comes as the Son. The Infinite and Eternal encounters us in our frailty in such a way that we can actually reject or accept his offer. The Sovereign Ruler of all comes to us, sacrificing himself for us, humbling himself for us, that we might experience fulfillment as real and free creatures.

Whatever is consistent with Christ is biblical. Whatever is less than or contrary to the fact and character of Christ is biblical only because it mirrors us as we are. Quite often the Bible so reveals us. Whereas the self in an ordinary mirror sees only the reflection of the actual self, the X-ray powers of the biblical mirror expose hidden faults. In its light, what may seem whole and healthy on the surface appears as sick and dying.

The Bible presents two kinds of truth: the truth of life as it is, neither idealized nor debunked; and the fuller truth not only of God's judgment on us but also of God's purpose for us. Basically, therefore, we may think of the Bible as the agent of salvation. It minors in theory and majors in practice; biblical truth lives. It rejects neat intellectual formulas in favor of simple stories of ordinary life. Biblical sermons have as their texts not great lines but great lives. Biblical preachers show our lives in all our inadequacies that they may lead us to the kind of life that alone satisfies and fulfills the highest and best in us.

(3) The Bible is a book of power. Wherein lies its power? *The power of the Bible is the Holy Spirit.* Only when we see the ways of the world according to the mind of Christ by the power of the Spirit does the Bible become alive. Then theory becomes living direction and direction becomes divine enabling. The Holy Spirit is love, for God is love, but the Spirit is more especially the power of the reality of love. He is a relation of power, for God as love is the source of all power.

The Holy Spirit is God as love, first in his own self, then in the community of those who receive him. The power of the Spirit is the power of the right relation to God. The power of the Spirit is the power of fellowship. Those who have displayed the fullest power to lift the world toward God are the ones who, feeling God within them, have thrown their lives wide open to the needs of the world. Thus true power is God's power and God's power is the power of love.

We do not read the Bible aright until we receive this power from above to live the Christian life within. As Augustine once intimated, philosophers may see the ideal way to live and yet lack the power to walk in it. Only the Spirit of power can thaw our hearts by his being love, can light our minds by his being love. Biblical power comes from living in the Spirit for the inclusive fellowship of concern for the common good. Men never acquire the mind of Christ apart from the power of the Spirit.

Christian faith, then, is biblical faith; it also is conviction. Whereas the Bible is on the side of truth, Christian conviction is on the side of trust. Truth and trust have to be wedded for Christian experience to be full and real. Christian conviction comes from the reading, accepting, and living of the Bible.

Christian conviction is no mere belief that something is or has happened. It is not faith *in* God, *in* Christ, *in* the Bible, or *in* any one or any thing. Christian conviction is direct "trusting" God. When Christian conviction is full and strong, it is no longer a believing *that* God will do something, for it is a confident "I believe *thee,* O Lord." When Christian conviction ripens to maturity, it is never a matter of believing *that* God can, or *in* God's faithfulness, but rather a direct "Thee I trust, O God of eternity, of the world, and of my life." Faith at its center is never a believing *that* or *in,* but simply and clearly believing God.

This does not mean that the Bible, history, and thinking have no place, or that they necessarily get in the way of personal faith. The previous section affirmed the place of the Bible as truth at the heart of Christian faith. We need its steady truth. However, when the Bible makes us face backward and not up, we are misled. Because God gave us the Bible, we now can know biblical faith. Because God came in Jesus Christ, we now can know him as the personal Spirit who is holy love. Because the Church was born on Pentecost, we now can have the new experience of Christian community. Because the Holy Spirit did come, we now can let him come into our lives.

The Bible should not shut God out as someone who once came and who once spoke; the Bible should rather open for us the way to heaven and home where we meet the Author of our biblical faith and rejoice in his presence. The Bible should make us look up to God in prayer and in devotion, in service and in friendship, and not merely back to the lives of others who once upon a time knew service and prayer. The Bible is not a "once-upon-a-time" book, but the book of present meeting with the living God and with his loving will. *Its truth must become trust in us.*

Jesus Christ demands our trust not merely as someone who came, taught, worked miracles, died for us, and rose victorious over death. Jesus Christ requires that we confront him now. Jesus Christ is God's presence in a human being as holy love. God came as light in Jesus Christ. God himself came to us in the fullness of time. Such a fact is crucial for knowledge, for faith, and for life. Nevertheless he came in Jesus as Son in order that we through grace and faith might find newness of life and become sons of the living God.

The Son came and keeps coming. Christ is God in man as holy love who wants to be the hope of glory in us. Christian conviction becomes real when biblical faith becomes personal trust. It is born when Christ is formed by grace and faith in our hearts. Christian conviction comes as the power of God for salvation through the Christian community, the holy fellowship of universal love that is the Church; and it arises when the Holy Spirit possesses our lives. Christian conviction does not depend mainly on our effort to believe; rather it is the faith made real in us because of a new Spirit.

II

Our commitment is to God. No one and nothing less than God can ever hold our full allegiance. God is the Creator of our lives; he alone can give us full reality as persons. We are made for God and in the depths of our lives we cannot deny that fact. We are satisfied only when his presence fills our lives. "Satisfy God if you would satisfy yourself," advised Père Jean-Nicolas Grou.

Our commitment, too, is to God's guidance. God has a plan for the universe; for the nations; and for each life. God never guides us in such a way as to make puppets or babes of us. We are free to choose; in fact we must choose. Constantly God confronts us with choices. When we choose aright, God shapes the plan of our lives for harder and better choices. When we choose wrongly, God works our plans around, making us face up again to the choice from which we ran away. God sees and knows what we need individually and collectively, and provides plans that further the good of all. The more we commit ourselves to God's will and keep doing so, the freer we become to choose the good. The more God works in us both to will and to do, the more we are truly ourselves and ready for real choosing.

Our commitment, too, is to a world in need. God cares for all; he longs to give spiritual, mental and physical help to all. He is concerned with the moral and social welfare of everyone. Biblical faith believes deeply enough in God's concern for all men to enter that concern. When our convictions "click" in God, they also click in regard to man. Our loyalty to God begets allegiance to man. Our liberty in God becomes freedom for man. Our surrender to God becomes self-giving for man. Our acceptance of God's guidance for our lives includes acceptance of his guidance into paths of help to others. Christian conviction invites commitment. Faith turns belief into faithfulness.

Christian conviction breeds and bears assurance. Assurance is the work of God. God alone can truly assure the heart that all is right within. Man wants to be self-assured. He admires the man who is sure of himself. Yet man cannot assure himself. His self-assurance is vain. God alone is the final Master of life even as God alone is the full meaning for life. Man needs to be made right with God. Without such rightness man has no true assurance. Without God at the center of his life the depths of man's life are empty, his self-assurance is futile.

Assurance comes from being right with God in the biblical way. It comes from opening our lives to him who is the judge and savior of all men. It is the work of Christ. When we see what God has done in Jesus and let him have his way likewise with our lives, we find assurance. Assurance comes from finding the power of right community and communion in the Christian fellowship. Such rightness with the true Church for which we are made can alone unleash the power of an endless life. Assurance is the work of the Holy Spirit, for only uncreated Spirit can give full assurance to created spirit.

Wherever God is truly present, there is assurance. Lack of assurance is lack of the presence of God. God is present in temptations. Temptations can be overbearing in their insistence even while the sense of God's presence helps us overcome the temptations. Jesus was tempted while full of the Holy Spirit. Tempted, he gave evidence of God's presence and of the assurance that alone can truly answer the tempter.

III

The union of biblical truth and Christian conviction brings forth Christian experience. For Christian experience to be real, we must (1) be born again, (2) continue in prayer, and (3) walk in the way of Christ.

The Bible is emphatic on the point that every human being must be born again. There is no exception. To be human is to be set on self. To be human is to wander away from God, from whatever point we know him. We are not by our created nature children of God. We are created with a nature that, in our kind of world, grows up selfish. We live also in a world of strife and competition, not only for food and glory but for affection and acceptance. In this world, therefore, we spend most of our time fighting for self. We fight with nature to live and with people to get ahead. We may not know we are doing it. Most of our fighting may be indirect. Nevertheless, by our very nature within our kind of world, we spend most of our lives trying to survive, to express the self, to impress others, and to prosper.

Without being born again we can never know God. We can have ideas of God which can be generally correct, as far as ideas go, but God is not met in ideas. Ideas can prepare for such meeting; they can help interpret that meeting. But God is met only in experience. The experience of God, moreover, is only in the Spirit. God is Spirit and the truth of meeting him is worship.

We cannot worship God unless we have the Spirit, or unless we are in the Spirit. God cannot give us his Spirit until we have heard who he is, until we are ready to give up our own spirit and to live a new life in his Spirit. When we see who God is and what he wants of us, we understand that God wants of us only what is good. Therefore, we repent of wasting our time in what is less than good, of sinning against God, and of doing little or nothing to make him known to those who need him. Regretting and wanting to be changed, we ask for God's forgiveness and for his new Spirit.

God meets us only when we are willing to give ourselves completely to him who has given and gives himself completely for us. The cross is the meeting place of God's own self-giving and man's self-giving, and both meet to save and to help the world. When God meets us at the cross, he gives us a new life. He lets us share in the resurrection of Jesus. We get new lives with him. We learn what it means to live in the Spirit. We begin to get Christian experience that combines biblical faith with Christian conviction.

We never have Christian experience apart from Christian conviction. In a way, Christian conviction must precede Christian experience. Unless we have heard and know what the Gospel is, we cannot receive it. As the Bible says, hearing comes from preaching and acceptance presupposes hearing. All the same, Christian conviction becomes strong and real only through growth in Christian experience. Genuine Christian experience therefore comes with the actual meeting of God and our surrender to him. To surrender to God is to become free. God wants our best. We surrender to him only to lose the false and fettered self. Being converted is being turned right.

We live in a way before we are born again. We live in darkness, however, and not in the light. We live in fear and not in peace. We live in conflict and not in love. We live enough to know that life can be better. We live enough to choose the better life.

It is held by some authorities that every infant has an emotional struggle at birth. Some babies resist birth more and some less, but all suffer some real struggle. Even so in the depths of our lives, we have our own struggle when confronted with decision for a new life. Some sinners fight harder than others. But when we accept rebirth, we find a new kind of life in which we are delivered from the darkness of our former life.

What happens in conversion is that we become real, genuine, straightened out, born into the kind of life for which we were created. We accept the kind of life for which we were originally born. We accept the spiritual life that is being right with God, the living of our lives in line with God's purpose for us.

The new life has to be sustained by prayer. Prayer is as necessary to spiritual life as breathing is to the physical life. The new life needs to grow and to be sustained by continual prayer in the same way as breathing has to go on all the time. True prayer is living in the light of God. True prayer is meeting God in spirit. Unless our spirits are "in the Spirit" we cannot keep living, much less grow spiritually. As Paul writes, "But you are not in the flesh, you are in the Spirit, if the Spirit of God really dwells in you. Any one who does not have the Spirit of Christ does not belong to him." (Romans 8:9.)

We often hear that prayer is an attitude. Our prayer is the deepest drive and strongest lure of our lives. Prayer is the way in which we set our lives toward God. No one can be continually conscious of his breathing. We have to work and sleep. We seldom think of the fact that we are breathing. In the same way prayer cannot be "without ceasing" if this means a deliberate, consciously cultivated praying. We can pray without ceasing only as we breathe without ceasing.

We pray with our lives more than with our lips. To be a Christian is to pray, to breathe toward God. To pray is to inhale God's atmosphere even as he inspires our lives. Such praying goes on during work and during sleep as well as during "times of prayer." Prayer is not only unconscious but also conscious.

Yet prayer is not only like breath to us, it is also like

food. We cannot eat all the time without being surfeited.
Instead, we eat at special times—either at planned times
or as we become hungry. Similarly we cannot pray all the
time. If we were to pray uninterruptedly, we could not
give our full attention to work or yield to the quiet rest
where attention stops and we are enfolded by the night.
To pray all the time as a deliberate act is as impossible
as to eat all the time. The prayer of the *heart* is like
breathing. It rises to God day and night without ceasing.
But the prayer of the *mind* is like taking nourishment.
We have set times for it or pray at particular times just
as we eat at mealtime or when we become hungry.

Prayer, both as breathing toward God and as taking
food, should be regulated by biblical faith. Prayer is according to the mind of Christ and in the power of the
Holy Spirit. To pray aright is to meet the God who is
completely, unconditionally, and unendingly love. True
prayer begins in the love of God, continues in the love
of God, is corrected by the love of God, and lets the love
of God use it in the full service of the love of God. Prayer
both as breathing and as eating is appropriating, trans-
mitting, and living the love of God.

Those who are born again, from above, and continue
in prayer, both as an attitude and as a practice, will also
walk in the way of Christ. Christian experience comes
from walking in the way of God's will. Biblical faith
needs trust in order for commitment to become experience.
Life produces Christian experience. Only as we live the
Christian faith with integrity can we keep trusting for
long. Experience allows God to become real; it makes

the mind of Christ relevant and important; it makes faith full enough to satisfy life.

To walk in the way demands intellectual integrity. Our mind walks in God's way when we make every thought obedient to Christ. When all our thinking means making truth consistent with God's holy love in Christ, we are walking in the way of truth. Then he who is the Truth can walk with us. We go his way and find that his way, though straight and narrow, is the way of intellectual satisfaction.

To walk in the way also demands constructive action for Christ. We can no longer live merely for ourselves. We are given genuine concern for others. We can no longer judge others as bad and as wrong while we, of course, do only what is right. Our concern for others makes us understand them, identify ourselves with them, and share their situation. We learn humility as well as helpfulness. Walking in the way demands personal giving of what we are and have. It demands our responsible participation in whatever good causes are for us the best channels of God's grace. It demands social concern and political responsibility.

Walking in the way, furthermore, means emotional satisfaction. It means that the self is right and therefore free. We do not substitute emotion for thinking or for action. Rather we set our emotions free to enjoy life within the cleanliness of integrity. We find God real who alone satisfies the soul. Only the pure in heart see him. The deeds of Christian experience kindle new and healthy affections. We are inclined to shortcircuit Christian experience and by confessing what we do not practice, burn out the wires of our lives. We have pumped up our feelings to justify what we say we believe. We have even tried to think we are living what we profess. We have filled our lives with emotional poisons by talking of the way without walking in it.

Christian experience is an exacting reality. When we fail to walk in the way, we prove the truth of the Christian faith by the unreality of our lives. When we do walk in the way of Christ, patiently and well, by God's grace and faith for every step, we discover that the Christian faith is fact and not fantasy.

Chapter II

The Christian Faith and Christ

The source for the Christian faith is Christ. He is the starting point. He is the rock foundation, strong enough to support the superstructure of faith.

"But who is Christ?" asks the bewildered layman.

Different people answer this question in different ways. Some treat him as a shibboleth to mumble over or, like a dose of distasteful medicine, a doctrine to swallow. Others think of him as the second name of a person whose first name was Jesus. Still others, puzzled by this confusion, think of him in terms of the confused and mixed feelings of their childhood. The less honest avoid thinking seriously about him.

Is there a true teaching about Christ? Can we know Christ as a historical fact? Can we know him as life itself? Countless people long for such knowledge. Is it possible to acquire it?

Some people have maintained that these questions are not of primary importance. For example, Mahatma Gandhi, the well-known Indian leader, once said:

From my youth upward I learnt the art of estimating the value of scriptures on the basis of their ethical teaching. Miracles had no interest for me. The miracles said to have been performed by Jesus, even if I had believed them literally, would not have reconciled me to any teaching that did not satisfy universal ethics. . . .

Jesus, to me, is a great world teacher among others. He was to the devotees of his generation no doubt "the only begotten son of God." Their belief need not be mine. He affects my life no less because I regard him as one among the many. . . .[1]

Gandhi's kind of approach to Christianity is not possible to the person who takes Christ seriously. The question of who he was and is cannot be avoided.

Dr. George Hendry of Princeton emphasizes this point of view in his penetrating book, *The Gospel of the Incarnation.*[2]

The Jesus-of-history movement is now a spent force. Three things helped to check its impetus. (1) The first was the increasing realization that the attempted simplification of the gospel was a gross oversimplification. It was impossible to set up an antithesis between the Jesus of history and the Christ of faith, because it is impossible to take the Jesus of history seriously without being led to the questions of traditional Christology. As Baillie put it, "The Jesus of history himself

[1]From *All Men Are Brothers,* p. 45.
[2]From *The Gospel of the Incarnation,* by George Hendry. Copyright 1958, by W. L. Jenkins, The Westminster Press. Used by permission.

can tell us that the Jesus of history is not enough."[3] (2)
The second was the rise of form criticism, which questioned
the assumption that a portrait of the historical Jesus could
be recovered from the Gospel records, since those records
had been shaped by the needs of the kerygma of the primitive church, and "the telling of the story of Jesus was Christ-
ological through and through from the start."[4] (3) The
third was the rise of the neo-orthodox theology, which re-
asserted the orthodox perspective upon the gospel in a chal-
lenging way.

D. M. Baillie maintains the same point of view when
he says that to take Christ seriously demands that he be
either more than Jesus or less than Jesus.

Despite the refusal of some even to face it, lest it become to them a source of confusion, the question remains:
Is there a clear teaching concerning Christ, at one and the
same time both biblical and central to the truth about
God and man? Can we find in him the clue to our origin,
nature, and destiny? In short, can we claim Christ as the
source of the Christian faith without sacrificing integrity
or intelligence?

This question defines the aim of the present chapter.
While the limitations of space preclude consideration of
the reasons for this affirmation, its implications can and
must be drawn.

Christ is the source not primarily for reason but for
faith and experience. But he is the source only for those
who in the Spirit are grasped and held fast by the Spirit.

[3]D. M. Baillie, *God Was in Christ*, p. 42. Faber and Faber, London, 1948.
[4]H. R. Mackintosh, *Types of Modern Theology*, p. 15. James Nisbet & Co.,
Ltd., London, 1937.

Faith sees Christ as truth. Faith's reason proclaims and elaborates this truth. Though the valid reasons for faith remain independent of their personal use, they are powerless until believers enlist their "eyes of faith" in the service of truth. But let us be careful to remember that faith is not true because we believe it, but rather we believe it because it is true. For faith that is Spirit-given, Christ is the truth that answers man's need.

There must, however, be the historical fact. If there is no fact, we have only the interpretation of imaginative illusions or delusions. There is much we do not know about the historical Jesus, yet there is enough trustworthy material for the venture of faith. We know the major outlines from birth to the resurrection.

We begin with the Incarnation. Christ is the fullness of God in the fullness of man in the fullness of time. In him the fullness of God dwelt bodily and more than bodily. In him the full presence of God and the full nature of man come together.

Christ as the Incarnation means the true indwelling of God himself in a human being. Incarnation means that in Jesus we meet God. It means that in him we see God at work. Performing his work in the transformation of men, turning them from what they actually are—lone, lost, and sinful—into what they actually can become— new creatures and members of a new community. Since familiarity and vain repetition have so often robbed these words of their cutting edge, we do well to take a fresh look at them. What do they really mean?

I

Jesus as the Son of God

As Nels Ferré emphasizes in his meaningful book, *Know Your Faith,* the New Testament offers three basic statements as to the nature of God: God is Spirit; God is our Father; and God is love. We begin our study of Christ with statements concerning God because the most important fact about Jesus is that he revealed God to man. He is Son of God. The meaning of this truth becomes clear in the light of the New Testament understanding of God as Spirit, as Father, and as love. Before we turn our attention to what God means in Jesus, however, we do well to look at the meaning of the word "son." In relation to God what does it mean to call Jesus "the Son"?

The declaration that Jesus is Son of God means that God himself, who eternally is outgoing, universal love, goes out of himself *as* a Son sent by his Father in order to create and to redeem. At the same time he remains himself—changeless love. God by his very nature *proceeds* to create and to make fellowship possible. Just as Tillich maintains that the expression Jesus as the Christ is preferable to Jesus Christ, so the expression God *as* Son may be preferable to God *the* Son. The Son is never a separate being independent of the Father, for the Father is truly present in and with the Son while the Son is ever present in and with the Father.

In other words the expression *the Son of God* simply means that the question of the meaning of God and the question of the meaning of Christ are the same. Thus, the meaning of God, to the Christian, is seen in the carpenter of Nazareth. Thus, the Christian does not begin with a concept or definition of God and then seek to understand how Jesus was the Son of God. Rather, the Christian begins with Jesus as the Son and in him discovers the nature of God.

When God is present as Son, he is present as Spirit. God is Spirit. Spirit is the reality that goes beyond the physical, the biological, and the personal. Aldous Huxley illustrates how difficult it is for modern man to understand the meaning of the word "spirit":

Miss Thriplow turned out the light, and kneeling down by the side of her bed, said several prayers aloud. She then got into bed, and lying on her back, with all her muscles relaxed, she began to think about God.

God is a spirit, she said to herself, a spirit, a spirit. She tried to picture something huge and empty, but alive. A huge flat expanse of sand, for example, and over it a huge blank dome of sky; and above the sand everything should be tremulous and shimmering with heat—an emptiness that was yet alive. A spirit, an all-pervading spirit. God is a spirit. . . . But God is a spirit. All the universes are one in the spirit. Mind and matter in their manifestations—all one in the spirit. All one—she and the stars and the mountains and the trees and the animals and the blank spaces between the stars and . . . and the fish, the fish in the Aquarium at Monaco. . . . And what fish! . . . Where was she? All things are one, ah yes, yes. All, all, all, she repeated. But to arrive at the realisation of their oneness one must climb up into the spirit.[5]

What makes sense to us when we try to think, "God is Spirit"? To say that God is Spirit means that he is beyond

[5]From *Those Barren Leaves,* Copyright 1948 by Harper & Brothers. Used by permission.

all our kinds of reality and that indeed we depend on him who is both more and other than we. God as Son is Spirit and, as such, mystery. We human beings can never know God in his eternal depths. We can know him only as he has revealed himself on our levels of reality and understanding. He is truly love, for instance, but God as love is not comparable to man as love. He is that and, also, what no eye has seen or ear heard or any imagination grasped. Paul continually emphasized this mysterious aspect of the gospel.

Often God never becomes real to us because we insist on being able to explain and predict him in human terms. Such a god is not the true God. God is never a thing or a being among other beings within our world of experience. He is rather the One from whom our world comes, by whom we gain birth and freedom, under whom we live and work, and to whom our lives shall return for judgment and salvation. We cannot remove Spirit from God without denying his mystery.

When we say God as Son comes as Spirit, we mean that he is not limited to, or by, our world, though all the while he gives meaning and structure to the workings of the world. The mystery of God came in Jesus Christ in matchless fullness. Hence the man who sees no mystery in Jesus Christ may have either ambitious eyes or a cowardly heart; if he does not look for too much, he settles for too little. He seeks in Jesus a finality history cannot give; reason cannot penetrate the depths and shadows of mystery. The light that shines through God in Christ illumines our darkness even while the light itself remains for us mystery. We need to make clear that mystery is not the mere absence of knowledge. Rather, at heart mystery is light too bright for us.[6]

The Son of God, as Spirit, raises for us some tremendous questions: Who is he who always is? How can thought fathom him? What is eternity like for the Eternal? How can God be himself and yet create that which is not himself? How can Spirit make that which is genuinely new? How can the future become? What makes it possible for God to communicate with what is not himself and even with what is imaginably different in kind? How can the sinless love the sinner, come in and dwell with him, and by his power remake him? We must not let words hide wonder from us. The Son of God as Spirit beyond words kindles wonder and awe even by the mystery of what is told us.

God is not only Spirit, but is also personal. Again, it is better to say personal than *a* person, for God does not have a personality like ours. As personal he is trinity. The consciousness of God, if we dare describe it, is neither just like that of a single human being nor a kind of collective consciousness. God is neither a solitary being nor a group. Such reality we cannot picture. Such experience is beyond our kind. Such is the nature of God as personal spirit. For this reason it is wrong to speak of the personality of God. God is rather the Spirit who by his own inner nature experiences threeness as well as oneness. Christian theologians for historic reasons and for want of better terms have

---

[6]See *Mystery and Meaning in the Christian Faith,* by Hugh T. Kerr, for further discussion of this topic.

called these three aspects of God's nature "persons" and the total God a "trinity."

God is definitely personal. We pray to him as Father. We love him as Friend. We ask his advice as Counselor. We feel his presence in history as Son. To say God is personal means that he has self-consciousness; that he has personal experience; that he plans, acts, loves, and is loved; that he knows, cares, and helps. It means that he pays attention to the world's needs, takes initiative in the creative advance of history, and answers our prayers according to his fuller understanding both of our needs and the best ways to meet them.

This personal God, who made heaven and earth and has raised up prophets for his people, came himself in Jesus as the Christ. What became personal in human experience was not an impersonal word but the Personal Word. Even more, the personal in man becomes mature and real only as the personal God fulfills and possesses man. Our tendency to say God but think Jesus is not only natural but proper. Jesus as the Christ is primarily the eternal Son who for our sake becomes man that we might know the only true God. We now know, therefore, the mysterious Spirit as the dependable personal Spirit whose character and face we see in his true human appearance in Jesus. In line with the many stories told to illustrate this truth, God has actually put on a face in Jesus as the Christ.

God is the personal Spirit who is holy love: this is the declaration of the New Testament. Jesus is the Son of God who is love. Christ-love characterizes the personal

Spirit. Christ-love never seeks its own. Always outgoing, it acknowledges no barrier and allows no condition to limit its activity. God's love is the universal love that breaks down barriers and builds up community. It is love that can never end and can never fail. It is steadfast love that cannot deny its own nature. Though all God's children turn faithless, God remains faithful for he cannot deny himself. His best name and his true character is love.

Even so, God's kind of love is hard to define. Shaun Herron, former editor of the *British Weekly,* illustrates this when he writes the following concerning his early experience:

I was brought up in a religious environment that was rigid, bigotted, and arrogant. The young in that place shed the faith of their fathers and began to look for something a good deal more profound and sophisticated. I remember that after I had thrown off the religion of the community in which I lived, I found myself, to my horror and by accident, in the dining room of a Christian Endeavor Holiday Home. I remember the disdain with which I read an inscription on the table napkins, "God is love." And the only thing I could think about it was that surely they had something more important to say. The young are arrogant and often stupid. I have often thought since then about this with embarrassment, for the practice of Christian love is the most dangerous and the most painful thing. And the simple statement that "God is love" is of all statements the most revolutionary in the Christian vocabulary, revolutions within persons and revolutions within communities.[7]

Jesus as the Son of such love taught it in parable and proverb. He illustrated it in healing and helping. He

[7]From *The Upper Room Chapel Talks.* Used by permission.

spoke of God as a father who welcomes home his wayward son and as a shepherd who seeks until he finds his last, lost sheep.

In his teaching, the first commandment calls for love to God, and the second for love to neighbor. He defined love with a parable in which a master pays the laborers in his vineyard according to need and not desert.

In his life he demonstrated love by going to the cross. Recall the story from World War I of a cassock-clad Jesuit walking over the field of battle, following a hand-to-hand conflict, holding aloft a crucifix and crying to the wounded and the dying, "Look, men, God loves like that." Even more, he proved love by rising from physical death.

That Jesus was Son of God means that in him the personal Spirit who is holy love became ruling in human history. Ruling not in terms of human success and power, but as the deep and moving force of a love that still hangs on the cross—a cross we can neither deny nor defeat.

II

Jesus as the Son of Man

Jesus was not only fully God in the sense that the true God, the personal Spirit who is holy love, actually lived in him. He was also as human as we are, indeed more so. Though he participated in our human problems and weaknesses, he was more human than we because he became related to God in such a way as to bring humanity to maturity. We are made for God so that only when God himself becomes the center of our lives can we be

truly and fully human. Since the center of Jesus' life was
the Son of God, he became in a fulfilling and true sense
the son of man. By growth and by learning obedience
through suffering and by the presence and power of the
Son of God in him the human *man* Jesus became man.
Thus God became man, the Word became flesh.

However, we must not forget that Jesus as a human
being was mortal, fallible, and victoriously human. He
was mortal; by that we mean he was made. Jesus as a
human being was born as are other men. His human
personality originated in time. We can date his birth and
set our calendars, at least roughly, by it. Jesus grew not
only physically, but mentally, socially, morally, and
spiritually.

The biblical record is clear on this point. He grew
before God and men. He grew in wisdom and stature.
He grew in obedience, learning it through suffering. He
grew through temptation and by the conquest of temptation. He grew through prayer and through companionship
with God in prayer. He demonstrated the magnitude and
genuineness of his humility in his refusal to call good
anyone but God. He recognized explicitly and thankfully
that it was God himself, his own Father, who did the work
in him, and that he as a human being apart from God
could do nothing. As son of man he felt complete depend-
ence on the Son of God.

Jesus had both a human will and human desires. We
do not say this because he became hungry and grew weary
or because he experienced keen disappointment, so evi-
dent in his reaction to his disciples for their failure to

understand him and to the religious leaders for their hard-
ness of heart. We say it because he experienced moral
and spiritual struggles throughout his entire life. Whether
precipitated by the refusal of Jerusalem to receive him or
by his persecution at the hands of uncouth men even to
death, the shock of rejection catapulted him into the
throes of tension. Because all he asked of life was the
chance to tell men of the goodness and faithfulness of God
his Father, he could not avoid a feeling of shock and hurt
at their response.

He had to wrestle with his inner self both in the wilderness and in the Garden. He was conscious that his own
will by its natural inclination was not identical with the
will of God. Therefore he had to cry, while battling unto
blood, "Not my will, but thine be done."

Recall again the broad outline of his life. Jesus, an ob-
scure Jewish carpenter, felt himself summoned by his
heavenly Father to a mission for mankind. He faced
courageously the manner in which his call was to be fulfilled. A simple reading of the temptation experiences—the
turning of the stones into bread, the leap from the pinna-
cle of the temple, the bowing down and worshiping the
forces of evil—fills one with a feeling of the awful in-
tensity and agony of the struggle. Yet Jesus was able to
recognize the real conflict involved, the basic impulse of
the self to do good. One by one he rejected the various
forms the self-drive takes. Jesus was willing to really trust
God.

There followed the years of ministry, a ministry of healing love. The scriptural record states it simply, "He went

about doing good," and doing good in such a way that he called attention not to himself but to God.

Toward the close of his life there came again the test of love. In Gethsemane on his knees with the darkness about him and in the insecurity of enemy territory, he sought for the final knowledge of truth in the way that the Father's will must be done. He had just risen and come from a fellowship feast during which he set aside his garment and, girded with a towel and basin, had washed the feet of his quarrelsome disciples. Both in the menial service which he had just performed, and in the awful stuggle in the Garden, Jesus revealed a willingness to really trust God.

Then in the final scene, bowing to the powers that be, receiving the taunts and jeers of the multitude, he accepted the physical and mental anguish of death.

Yes, Jesus was mortal and partook of our mortal struggles. The record assures us that the Incarnation was real, that God became actual man. But the most important truth about Jesus, the human being, concerns neither the fact of his mortality nor his fallible experience. It has to do with the fact that he conquered death and, being made perfect, became the pioneer and perfecter of our faith. The Bible leaves no room for doubt on this point of its message concerning the Christ. The Son of God had to enter our human life and assume our whole plight as human beings in order to save us. An ancient church father, Gregory of Nazianzus spoke truly when he said: "What was not assumed was not healed." God in Christ assumed our mortality. He took on himself our death, our ignorance, and our sin. He entered within our weakness and our depravity that by his strength and sinlessness he might cancel the power of sin and death and release us forever from their power. The Son of God lived, died, and rose from death that he might make a living way for us to the Father through his own flesh.

The whole point of the story of Jesus is that God who is holy love so loved us from eternity that he created us, prepared the way for the coming of his Son, and then sent his Son that we through him might be saved. God saves us by entering into our humanity to enable us from within to get rid of our sin, fear, and failure. He reveals the knowledge of salvation by entering into human life and illuminating us from within. God also enables man to become victorious over all his enemies by his coming in Jesus as light and life, living, dying, and rising from death. God first enabled the man Jesus, by the presence of his own Son in him, thus fulfilling his humanity, to achieve victory over sin, law, ignorance, fear, finitude, and death.

The crucial point of the story is that he did it in our stead, that we, seeing the Son of God in the Son of man, might accept God's way of working, forgiving, and rising to newness of life within our own lives. The eternal Son of God became man that mankind might know and be saved by the Son of man.

III

Jesus as Savior

Jesus is not only Son of God and Son of man; he is also and primarily Savior. Our interest in Jesus stems not so much from a rational demand of the head as the crying need of the human heart. Abstract theories and learned theologies may even hide from us him whom God sent for our salvation.

Tolstóy, with his penetrating insight, points out what it means to move from the analytical to the personal in his story, *The Death of Iván Ilích*. Iván is an ordinary man, with ordinary hopes and desires. He is married and has a family; he is rather a likable fellow. One day he falls from a ladder. The accident seems trivial and he tries to forget about it. But the pain in his side persists. He goes from doctor to doctor seeking help. No diagnosis seems to help.

Iván Ilích was interested in but one question, and that was, whether his situation was dangerous, or not. But the doctor ignored this irrelevant question. From the doctor's standpoint, this question was idle and not subject to consideration; there existed only a weighing of probabilities—between a floating kidney, a chronic catarrh, and the disease of the caecum. . . . From the doctor's résumé Iván Ilích drew the conclusion that things were bad, and that it was a matter of indifference to him, the doctor, and, for all that, to all people, but bad for himself.[8]

Analysis is good but the crucial question remains, "Is there help for the patient?" If analyzing the life of Jesus keeps us from seeing his life as a whole, God's mighty Christ-deed for our salvation, we have indeed exchanged our birthright for a mess of pottage. Analysis fails of its purpose if it does not show us how God's coming in Christ

---

[8]Translated by Leo Wiener and copyright 1904 by Dana Estes & Company.

must be followed by his coming in us. If it does not show us how Christ can and must dwell in our hearts, the faith becomes meaningless.

As Savior, Jesus reveals to us the sin both of self and of society. The light shows up the dark. Men did not know the utter darkness of sin until Jesus came. He exposed the current views of sin in all their inadequacy. He did not think of sin simply as the perpetration of an evil deed or a violation of the law but rather as a kind of life, as a quality and direction of living. Before sin becomes sins or acts, it is a state of the self. Jesus as the true self showed up the false self. Jesus as the love that is the light of the world and the law of life laid bare the dark drives of human nature and uncovered the lack of love that causes lawlessness. Before the appearance of Jesus, men had never been forced to face the merciless floodlight of God's holy, universal, unfailing love. They did not know what God demanded that they be and how God expected them to act. Therefore, when Jesus came, he swept away their last refuge of using ignorance as an excuse for sin.

God's love, also, reveals as inadequate a so-called love that is really only charity. Dr. Herron illustrates this in the telling of his moving story concerning the man who created Mau Mau in Africa, Jomo Kenyata.

He is a man of real genius, a man of tremendous character and overwhelming personality. In any society of any color he would have stood out among men. Our missions in Africa gave him the chance of an education. He went in time to London and studied in the University of London. His experiences and life in England made him into a middle-class Englishman. Out of love, Christian love and the gifts of Christian missions, he went back to Kenya; but there in his own land we denied him the status of a middle-class Englishman. We denied him the opportunities of a middle-class Englishman. Once again he was just Kenyata, the native. All the tastes of an educated gentleman, all the aspirations of an educated gentleman—but none of the rights.

You and I would probably have done in that situation what he did. Our love was the thing that destroyed him because our love was "charity." It wasn't sufficiently creative; it wasn't sufficiently constructive. We set him up just to destroy him. What could he do? If we loved him only that we might make a model of our generosity out of him, then we created Mau Mau, full of hate and poison and murderous destructiveness, because we, the British Christians, could offer him only initial kindness and an opportunity to acquire skills and gifts that we would not allow him to use. When we Christians say that our love is our gift to the world, let us realize what a dangerous thing we are saying: how much it demands of us and how endless it is in its demands and its responsibility.[9]

The Savior of men, then, in the full light of God's living truth reveals both the fact and seriousness of our sin. He does so, however, only in order to save us. God sent his Son not to condemn the world but that the world through him might be saved.

God, moreover, has all the resources that are necessary for man's salvation. He has the resources by which he made man for himself. He who is Lord of lords has at his command the unemptiable resources to guide man to choose life rather than death, maturity rather than child-

[9]From *The Upper Room Chapel Talks*. Used by permission.

ishness, love rather than sin, the true self rather than the false self, God as Father rather than self as tyrant.

Before God created the world, he knew that man would be faithless and rebellious. God knew that man had to go his own way in order to become free and to mature. Sin was no surprise to God. Thus God also prepared the proper remedy for sin before he fashioned the foundations of the world. From the beginning, God put the cross at the center of the world's history.

God knew that man would never have power enough to save himself. He wanted man to be dependent on him and on others in order that man might find the joy of community. God wanted man to need God and his fellow man in order that only the divine society could finally fulfill life. Thus God purposed to save man through Jesus Christ.

God realized that only as he himself could enter fully into man's sinful situation and from within give man the power to overcome sin could man be saved. The healing medicine could only be God's life given freely in suffering for man, and man's life given freely in suffering back to God and through the power of God for man. Such is the meaning of Jesus as Savior.

Chapter III

The Christian Faith and Man

Our age finds man confused and baffled. He is suffering from what E. Stanley Jones has so aptly called, "the paralysis of analysis." If man is to be brought out of his present meaninglessness and despair, he must discover his true purpose and direction.

Fulton J. Sheen graphically portrays this when he writes:

They want to be whole again. They are sick of being thrown into a Darwinian pot to boil as a beast, or into a Freudian stew to squirm as a libido, or thrust into a Marxian sandwich to be squeezed between two conflicting slices of capital and labor. They want to possess that which makes them human, gives meaning to politics, economics, psychology, sociology: namely, the soul.[1]

The question arises, "What is man?" It is fairly easy to define man in some of his aspects such as the "biologi-

[1]From *Philosophies at War*, by Fulton J. Sheen. Copyright 1943 by Charles Scribner's Sons. Used by permission.

cal animal" of Darwin, the "psychological animal" of
Freud, the "economic animal" of Marx, and so forth.
Each view would give a partial insight into the nature of
man and as such would be helpful. But each view if considered as the whole view of man would be a distortion.

Does, then, the biblical view of man allow for the com-
plexity of man? The biblical faith assures us that man is
made by God. Man is no accident or product of chance;
he is not haphazard creation; nor is he the product of a
perpetual evolution. Man is not the highest form of intelligence and meaning that we know. In the beginning God
created him.

The method of creation allows for man to be part of
the natural order. There is no doubt man is made from
the dust and is of the earth earthy. He is a part of God's
long history of creation. He belongs to the process of biological development just as the earth belongs to that of
geological evolution. Man is part of the grand thrust of
natural history, which is God's way of working. But the
dust never became man until God breathed his spirit into
it.

Thus, even though man belongs to the process of biological evolution, this is not meant to imply that man is
only animal. In *The Christian Understanding of Man,*
Robert Calhoun points out the differences involved in the
two views.

Man as animal is thought of more or less uncritically, in
lay circles, as at once a child of nature and its destined Lord.
In contrast to the traditional view of man as sprung directly
from a supernatural source, the tendency now current among

the modernist laymen is to think of man as part and parcel of the natural order arisen in the midst of it, not come down into it from above. Man thus viewed is not "the debris of Adam" created in the image of God and fallen into ruin, but the hero of a long upward climb which is still going on.[2]

The Bible clearly states that man comes from the dust but belongs to God because God breathed his spirit into him. God created him in his own image. This means that God created man for a special relationship. Man is made for fellowship with God. In order for man to be able to have fellowship with God, he was created as a personal spirit.

To say man is personal means that he is both conscious and self-conscious. He knows himself. The predicament and glory of man stem from his ability to be both a pleasure and a problem to himself. Man continually is beset by what Kierkegaard called "*Angst*," often translated "anxiety," a deep-seated anxiety. Consciously or subconsciously man is faced with the question, "What is going to happen to me?" Each man is aware that he is both a part of the world and also over against the world. Thus at times he feels at home and at ease and at other times he feels like an alien and ill at ease. Man is both conscious and self-conscious. He can recall the past and anticipate the future.

To be a person, also, means to be a responsible creature. Man has freedom of choice. He can make his own decisions. Even though his choices are weighted both from within and without, man has the power to postpone a present good for a greater good. Thus, freedom rests on

---

[2]The Oxford Conference Study Series for 1938, No. 2.

his back as both a precious privilege and a horrid burden.
A person can know the future and take thought for it or
he can grow weary from worry over it. He can rejoice in
what never happens or he can fret himself sick over it. A
person, in this sense, is really alone. This is the terrifying
part of being a person that drives some people to all kinds
of desperate acts in order to escape this aloneness. Some
seek to dominate others. Some allow themselves to be
dominated.

Raymond Ferris, rector of Christ Episcopal Church,
Nashville, Tennessee, reveals in his personal story how
easily this can happen.

One day, while upon my knees at my prayers in the church,
the vision of my wife, the idea of my wife, kept going back
through my head and disturbing my prayer. You know how
wandering thoughts are a curse to everybody who tries to
come to God upon his knees. Well, that day it was the idea
of my own wife; and finally I said, "Well, God, if she is going
to be so much in my mind, I will pray about her." So I gave
up everything else and prayed about her. I finally went
through what the mystics call "contemplating her before
God." I stood her out there and saw her before God until
finally I realized in the sight of God, while we are man and
wife upon earth, yet she is an individual before him. There
is a sense in which I infringe her individuality if I insist that
she is primarily related to me. She is not. She is primarily
related to God. She is a child of God; and she stands there
before him: and I have no right to dominate, or demand, or
in any way supersede that relationship. I must stand off. Do
you know the words of Kahlil Gibran how he said, "Let there
be spaces in your togetherness"?[3]

[3]From *The Upper Room Chapel Talks.* Used by permission.

The image of God in man is not only personal; it is also spirit. Spirit is God's own presence in man. Spirit is what leaves man still unsatisfied with only what this world has to offer. Spirit is man's restless search for God. In the familiar words of Augustine, "Thou hast made us for thyself and our souls are restless until they rest in thee." Spirit is man's emptiness apart from God. Spirit is what makes man creative, inventive, thinking of things beyond what he can see. Spirit makes it possible for man to meet God, to have conversation and communion with God.

The image of God shows man to be made for holy love and calls for the absolute right. Right relations, right actions, and right attitudes are necessary for man to be satisfied. To be sure man can evade what is right. He can numb his conscience and silence its voice in his conscious self. But the image continues to speak in the subconscious. Neuroses develop on the heels of man's repudiation of his moral strivings. Innumerable mental or physical breakdowns presuppose the breakdown of man's conscience as a conscious counselor for right. Man can no more get rid of the image of God than he can get rid of God. Any attempt to do so precipitates inner conflict or spiritlessness. Life loses its meaning. It becomes empty.

Jean Paul Sartre in his dramatic style reveals this emptiness of man without God in his play, *The Flies*. Orestes, the spokesman for Sartre's view, is disgusted because he has not become the well-rounded man he had hoped. Instead, life has become meaningless.

The tutor defends himself in this fashion.

You grieve me, my young master. Have all my lessons, all my precepts, the smiling scepticism . . . been wasted on your ears? . . . Did I not, from the very first, set you a-reading all the books there are, so as to make clear to you the infinite diversity of men's opinions? And did I not remind you, time and again, how variable are human creeds and customs? So, along with youth, good looks, and wealth, you have the wisdom of far riper years; your mind is free from prejudice and superstition, you have no family ties, no religion, and no calling; you are free to turn your hand to anything. But you know better than to commit yourself. . . . And yet you cavil at your lot![4]

Man is made for commitment. Therefore man cannot destroy the image. But man is also made to be free. Therefore God never gives ready-made answers to what is right. Conscience is relative in order for man to be free. Man must learn from his own experience and from the experience of others. He must compare his own experience with previous experiences and with the experiences of others. He must try to find out what is right by learning at home, at school, in church, from books and friends.

Conscience, then, never comes ready-made. The voice of conscience may not be the voice of God. Rather, it must be subject to enlightenment and growth. Christ, as the Bible says in 1 John 3:20, is greater than our conscience. Man's sense of right is from God and is absolute in its demands. Conscience, as Heidegger has implied, is the will to be guilty—to accept the guilt that we know will be ours.

---

[4]In *No Exit* translated by Stuart Gilbert. Copyright 1947 by Alfred A. Knopf, Inc. Used by permission.

Most people avoid taking this aspect of the Christian faith seriously. This does not invalidate its truth but rather underscores it. Joan of Arc, speaking to the weakling King of France, Charles VII, says:

"I have a message for you from God."

Charles replies, "I care not to hear it."

Joan proceeds, "Thou must listen though thy heart break with the terror of it."

To which Charles replies, "Let others have their belly full of fighting. All I want is to sleep in a comfortable bed and have a full stomach."

Then Joan declares, "You must listen, you are a child of a King and you cannot deny that."

So man is made in the image of God with a sense of right and oughtness that he cannot deny without life collapsing around him.

Man thus is related to God by creation and by the image of God in him. But man is also related to God by destiny. God one day will sum up all things; some day he will complete each life as well. Soren Kierkegaard relates the story of a man who becomes thinner day by day; he is wasting away. "He does not suffer from lack of food. Rather, his illness is due to the fact that he eats out of season, eats without being hungry, uses stimulants to arouse a little bit of appetite, and in that way he ruins his digestion, fades away as if he were suffering from lack."[5] Man can go on living in such a way that he

---

[5]From *Attack Upon "Christendom."* Copyright 1944 by Princeton University Press. Used by permission.

never really faces the reason for his existence until after death. But this simply postpones the problem of life for in the end man is related to God.

In our relation to the Father we are by the very image in us eternal. In ourselves we are not immortal. Quite the contrary! But God the eternal chooses to be at the center of our lives. We have no life apart from him and by him. Since he calls us into everlasting life, we can be assured of it. In this life we go to sleep and without taking conscious thought are awakened each morning to newness of life. At the time of death we fall asleep as human beings, only to be waked up to the resurrection life by the Spirit who calls us beyond the grave even as he called us into life on this side of the grave.

It needs to be pointed out that God the Father never appears in visible form. He is beyond any such appearance. God in himself is invisible. Our creation in his image means that we, too, are truly invisible. The true self is never seen. The true self cannot be seen. We can see only the appearance of the self. The real self is beyond all study. He is even beyond self-study. The most real self is mainly in God's heart for us. He comes to us as we appropriate him from God in our living. The self is life's real mystery in this world. No psychology can find him, for he cannot be discovered by observation. The solitude of the self is an irreducible dimension of human life no matter how completely that self seems to be contained in its social milieu. William Barrett in his study in existential philosophy, *Irrational Man,* dramatically points out this hidden self experienced by man.

But the worst and final form of alienation, toward which indeed the others tend, is man's alienation from his own self. In a society that requires of man only that he perform competently his own particular social function, man becomes identified with this function, and the rest of his being is allowed to subsist as best it can—usually to be dropped below the surface of consciousness and forgotten.[6]

Our creation in the image of the Son in us stands for the unique individuality of each one of us. Each person is absolutely precious to God and forever in his keeping, for each person is marked eternally with the image of God's Son. The image is a sign and token that God is faithful eternally in his love for each and every child; for God cannot deny himself.

Man is also created in the image of the Spirit. The Spirit stands for the plurality in God. God is by nature community as well as individuality. There would not be in creation both individuality and community unless God himself were both. Therefore, all stress on the individual as such defies God. All stress on freedom of the individual apart from the community revolts against God the Creator.

God as Spirit accounts for the reality of the Church. The true Church, the Church within the organization and for which the organization exists, is of God. For the true Church is community in the Holy Spirit. The true Church defines man's existence as a social creature. Man is made to be fulfilled in the Church. Apart from such fulfillment there can never be any salvation. Thus, Cyprian, an early

---

[6]From *Irrational Man* by William Barrett. Copyright © 1958 by William Barrett. Reprinted by permission of Doubleday & Company, Inc.

church father, could say, "Outside the church there is no salvation." To find and accept the Spirit is to find and accept the work of the Church of Christ.

To be sure, the organization falls short of the reality of which it is the needed vehicle. Nor are all in the organization by any means in the Church. Doubtless, too, there are many in the Church of Christ, in the reality of their acceptance of him and of the Holy Spirit, who have never understood the reason for the organized church and therefore have not joined it.

Nevertheless the full truth of the Christian faith is that men are made, at the center of their lives and at the core of God's plan for them, for the inclusive, holy fellowship which is the Church. By the very presence of the image of God in man, one part of which is the Spirit, man in order to be saved must find and become part of the Church. The Church, on the other hand, is made in the image of God the Spirit and must therefore be judged by the extent to which it is completely open to God, is all outgoing to men and is entirely inclusive in its invitation and outreach. Man and the Church belong together within the plan and purpose of God the Son and God the Spirit in whose image they are created and alone fulfilled.

Thus man belongs to God by the nature of his being, his creation, the image of God in him and his being made for final fulfillment only in God. This reality is structured at its heart by God being trinity himself. By God the Father man is eternally the invisible spirit, created for companionship with God; by God the Son man is a unique individual who is absolutely precious in the heart of God; and by God the Spirit man is a social being who can reach his maturity and fulfillment only within the Church which is the eternal purpose God purposed in Jesus Christ before he made the earth.

Man, being fashioned in the image of God, should seek to develop three basic aspects of his life, each stemming from his relation to the trinity.

The Father stands for character. In his likeness man should have character. We are here to grow character. There can be no family or community life without character. Without character in the lives of men, life becomes irrational. Rationality demands that we can depend upon people. To give every indication of making a big show and failing to perform reveals a lack of character. Many of the ills of the world can be traced back to the lack of character in man.

Where character is lacking, the will to power, the will to recognition, the will to self-satisfaction, or some similar drive will take over. Instead of man being in control, some demonic drive controls him to make havoc of his life. Dostoevski continually pointed this out in his writings. The most penetrating of these writings may have been his story, *Crime and Punishment*. Dr. Barrett calls attention to this insight in the following passage:

The hero, Raskolnikov, is the alienated intellectual—alienated at once from the collective body of mankind and from his own being. Hungry and solitary, he spins out of the bowels of his own reason a Nietzschean theory (before Nietzsche) of the Superman who through his own superior daring and strength rises above all ordinary moral codes. Then to put his theory to the test he kills an old pawnbroker. But the criminal is unequal to his crime: Raskolnikov's theory has not reckoned with his own self, and the guilt over his crime brings on a breakdown. Precisely the feelings that had been repressed in this intellectual—the ordinary human horror at the taking of life—erupt and take their revenge. What drove Raskolnikov to the crime had nothing to do with the justifications he fabricated to himself: He reasoned, "I am poor, this old pawnbroker is a louse; by killing and robbing her, I can relieve my mother of the awful strain of paying for my studies"; but in fact, as he admits finally to the girl Sonia, he killed in order to prove to himself that he was not a louse like the ordinary run of mankind. . . . The will to power is weakness as well as strength, and the more it is cut off and isolated from the rest of the human personality, the more desperate, in its weakness, it can become. Thus Raskolnikov kills out of insecurity and weakness, not out of an excess of strength: he kills because he is desperately afraid that he is nobody. And indeed he is, for his mind has so lost touch with the rest of him that he is not properly speaking, a self.[7]

We must be aware of a genuine danger in stressing character. Man at best is not self-made but God-made. He is not the dependable so much as he is the dependent, the one who needs God and trusts him. To boast of human character is folly. Nevertheless character is Christian. Character is not in place of God but the very place of God in our lives. Character means consistency of conduct. The dependability of a Christian is not his goodness over against and compared with God's, but is rather the presence of the goodness of God in man.

When man has seen God's light in Christ or even the natural light of conscience that shines in all men, and accepts the will of God to the best of his knowledge, the faithfulness of God itself then demands that man grow character. There is, of course, likely to be false growth and many a slip, and there is a likelihood, too, of inertia that slows down or even stymies growth. Insofar, however, as man genuinely understands and accepts God in Christ, he finds the Father, and should reflect the faithfulness of the Father by growing Christian character.

The Father also stands for self-sufficiency before all relations. He is himself and is not dependent on his creation. Even so the Christian should have his sufficiency in God and therefore not be dependent upon human judgments. He should stand strong in God above social fears and social favors. A man should grow character through courage. But there is no growth of character without discipline. A. J. Wilson, minister in the United Church of Canada, relates an interesting personal experience.

Father ordered me upstairs. Crawling slowly up in hope that I might hear some repentance on my mother's part, I heard her say to Father, "Now don't be too hard on that boy, James, for after all I suppose it is only human nature." "Human nature," my father answered, "is all right but it can be improved, and I am going to assist in the improvement."[8]

Character is grown by accepting discipline both from without and within. Yet character as such is never fully Christian. The most important thing about God is not that he always remains the same. He does, for God is everfaithful Love. But God is not self-concerned. God is not self-sufficient in the sense that nothing matters to him

___

[8]From *The Upper Room Chapel Talks.* Used by permission.

except for him to remain the same. God is not the self-same in the sense that he causes and knows no change. God has a perfect character in remaining self-same as God, but God is Father. He has relations, even though he is before and above them and not dependent upon them. They depend upon him. The character of his conduct, however, is creative concern.

"In the beginning God created. . . ." God is Creator. The Creator causes and knows change. He who is the source of all riches produces new ones by creation and glories in the creative new. "And God saw that it was good."

Man who is made in the image of the Son and who lives only by being related to God through the eternal Son should express this reality by becoming creative. Character apart from creative interests is dull regularity and borders on boredom. Creativity gives zest to life. It touches life with creative adventure. Character is needed for creativity. The creative spirits of the world have had a steadiness of purpose. They may have defied the customs of civilization and broken rules in every realm of life. Yet they have been driven on by something they had to see, had to say, had to create. Their lives became identified with their creations.

General Charles Carpenter, chief of Chaplains, United States Air Force, emphasizes this creative adventure in his reflection on the life of George Washington.

Living in Washington as I have over the past few years, whenever I am in the city on Memorial Day, I make a patriotic trek down the Potomac to Mount Vernon. Mount Vernon is a place of mystery to me. Stand there if you will on the portico and look across the lawn beyond the Potomac to the rolling hills of Maryland. Close your eyes momentarily and realize that long years ago a man lived here who possessed great wealth, servants to do his bidding, acreage that produced the needs for his home and made it possible for him to have financial wealth with which to do the things that he desired to do. A man of wealth and a man of leisure lived in this home, Mount Vernon.

One day there galloped a horse into the yard of that home. A man dismounted and said to Mr. Washington, "Mr. Washington, your neighbors to the North are uniting to overthrow the rule of England. They would like to have you join them." And then the mystery took place. A man possessed of wealth and of leisure and of security mounted his horse and rode North. He rode far North to take command of a ragtag Continental Army which fought its battles and made its retreats until one day it found itself in the midst of a winter encampment outside the city of Philadelphia in a place called Valley Forge—snow on the ground, the coldness of the days, many ill-clad, ill-supplied. I wonder if Mr. Washington at that time did not think of Mount Vernon? He had but to mount his horse and ride South and enter the comforting and secure bonds of that estate. He would have found those who would do his bidding, plenty of food, leisure, and wealth. Mr. Washington left Mount Vernon to ride to near disaster, but out of the experience came a new America, a new America brought into being by dedicated men of which he was one. Washington was a man who placed the interest of the group above and beyond his personal thoughts of security and safety and leisure.[9]

Each Christian is challenged to that type of dedication to Christian living, leaving behind what he has, that

---

[9]From *The Upper Room Chapel Talks*. Used by permission.

which makes him feel secure and safe, and in the name of Christ going out into the area in which he lives in creative adventure.

Creativity is not for the few. All are related to the Son. All are made in the image of the Son. Each person needs to create. In a very simple illustration of this truth, a certain cake mix nearly went bankrupt when all the housewife had to do was add water. It did not sell. They brought it back to the market with the direction of adding an egg then stir. Allowing for some small creativity, the cake mix is selling very well. The urge and drive for "do it yourself," also, points out this truth. Creativity is not mostly a matter of producing universally known works of art, literature, or thought. Creativity is mostly the seeing for oneself the richness of life within the joy of contributing to the enrichment of life.

Each person sees and responds to a world all his own. Not even God invades that privacy of vision and response that makes man exactly himself. God is with each man but leaves opportunity for each man to be himself. It is a glorious privilege to be oneself: to see, to feel, to respond as no one has ever seen or felt or responded before. God is creative in each person and shares something of the zest of each man's creative response, but also leaves each man free to be a unique individual.

A Christian, then, ought to be particularly creative. He ought to have character as consistency of purpose. He ought also to receive the unity that makes his life orderly. He ought besides to experience the absolute uniqueness of his own self and the privilege of living. He ought thereupon to open his eyes wide to God's creation, sharing God's creativity. He ought to open his ears fully to the music around him, sharing God's creativity. He ought to let his spirit be freed by the presence of the Son to experience ever new worlds for himself, sharing God's creativity.

Dullness of life reveals a lack of faith. Boredom is sin. Meaninglessness reflects an inner illness. Worship, work, and play should all be carried on when the spirit of man receives true character from God as Father and creativity from God as Son.

Man made in the image of God as Father should show a Christian character, should reflect his creative power, and should exhibit the reality of concern. Character stands for steadiness; creativity stands for enriching change; but concern stands for God himself, for his very heart. God is love, the love who relates himself. The social in God is precisely love and the right social relation among men is precisely love.

A Christian is one who through his personal faith becomes more adventurous, more brotherly, more courageous, more decent, more enthusiastic than others. This in life may be the answer to Jesus' searching question, "What more are you doing than others?"

Chapter IV

The Christian Faith and Salvation

In a small town in Canada, the plays of William Shakespeare are continually being staged. Many visitors from the United States, as well as Canada, are drawn to see and hear these plays performed in almost flawless style.

The story is told of a visitor who was on his way to a performance of *Julius Caesar*. On his way, he asked the taxicab driver if he had seen any of the plays. The cab driver nodded in the affirmative. The visitor proceeded to ask if he had read any of the plays. The slow-speaking cab driver retorted, "After seeing my first play, I bought a book containing the plays of Shakespeare. I must say she sure acts much better than she reads."

The subject of this chapter is the atonement—how God saves. My own personal feeling, the few times I have tried to discuss this, has been that "she sure acts better than she reads."

The atonement seeks to explain how man, who is separated from God, can be brought back to God. When it comes to explaining this act in a neat formula, there is something here that seems to defy human explanation.

However, the truth in the doctrine of the atonement contains the answer to the deepest longing of the human heart, the longing for being at-one with God and the longing for a genuine change in our human nature. This is so central to the Christian faith that it needs to be made as intelligible as possible to every follower of Jesus Christ.

Robert McCracken, pastor of Riverside Church, New York, in one of his sermons raises the pertinent question, "Can Human Nature Be Changed?" He begins by telling this very dramatic story taken from Dick Sheppard.

Dick Sheppard used to tell a story about a man who sat drinking in a bar. He had been drinking for a long time. He had swallowed considerable quantities of liquor. And as he drank, he wept. He wept because he had wasted his life. He wept because he had failed to do his duty by his family. He wept because he had never appreciated his wife properly. He wept because somehow his good intentions always went wrong. But never mind, he told himself, this time it would be different. He would redeem the past and make up for everything. All, he resolved, would yet be well. He felt uplifted and noble at the very thought. His mind glowed with a genial assurance of virtue. Just then the bartender said, "Time, gentlemen, please"—*and he went home and swore at his wife*.[1]

Can human nature really be changed? Contrast the Dick Sheppard story with John Masefield's Saul Kane.

---

[1] From *Questions People Ask*. Copyright 1951 by Harper & Brothers. Used by permission.

Saul, rough, tough, uncouth fighter, finds himself half-drunk on Christmas night in a stuffy barroom. A Quaker lass enters. He insults her, shocking all who are present. She speaks to him. "Christ waits for you to knock." Saul is sobered. Stumbling out of the bar, he says to himself:

> I did not think, I did not strive,
> The deep peace burnt me alive;
> The bolted door had broken in,
> I knew that I had done with sin.
>
> I knew that Christ had given me birth
> To brother all the souls on earth,
> And every bird and every beast
> Should share the crumbs broke at the feast."[2]

Is Saul's experience true to life? The Christian faith maintains that human nature not only can but must be changed. Through trust in Jesus as the Christ, we can obtain forgiveness for our sins and a right relation with the Father. This new relation enables God to heal man of his sin, relieve him of that which enslaves him, and release him from the fear of death. In Christ, man becomes a new creature—human nature is actually changed.

Salvation involves two directions. The first is to have the right relation with God. The second is to have right relations with men. "You shall love the Lord your God with with all your heart, and with all your soul, and with all your strength, and with all your mind; and your neighbor as your self."

---

[2]From *The Everlasting Mercy.* Used by permission of The Macmillan Company.

How does man enter into a right relationship with God? The church has continually struggled to express this experience in meaningful terms. It may be helpful to consider briefly the major historical theories of salvation held by Christians. No one view has ever been universally accepted.

(1) The patristic theory dominated Christian thought for the first ten centuries, or until the time of Anselm. According to this theory, Christ's death and descent into hell was for the purpose of paying to the devil a ransom for the redemption of mankind from the power of Satan and hell.

In the Eastern church, John of Damascus (675-749) was one of the most discerning to hold this view. He wrote in mytho-poetic language which makes it difficult to translate his meaning to our day. We may also lack the depth to appreciate his deep feelings and insights.

John maintains that there are two aspects of our redemption which are one continuous process. The first aspect is the Incarnation whereby God takes on our human nature. God puts on a human face, becomes one with human nature, in order to defeat the devil fair and square. In God's victory, we all are victorious in the identity of the all in the one.

This can best be illustrated by the expression of the alumni when they exclaim of their college team, "We won our football game Saturday."

Incarnation deals mostly with taking on our human form. It would be disgraceful to be almost beaten and then have someone else take over for us. We would not then actually have won. Thus, according to John, God became human in order that humanity may win the victory.

The second aspect of our redemption is the atonement. If the Incarnation had been sufficient, the cross would not have been necessary; but it is. Sin, death, and the devil are defeated through the cross.

John pictures the devil in grotesque symbols as a great fish and Christ as the bait. The devil tries to swallow Christ, he gets caught on the hooks of Christ's divinity and ends by vomiting up all he (the devil) has devoured.

This is mytho-poetic language. What does it mean? The devil is symbolic of the forces of evil, pride, hatred, and so forth. Christ drew the powers of evil as a magnet. In order to continue these forces would have to destroy the magnet. As they sought to do so, the powers were destroyed by the new life-giving power. This new life was powerful enough to affect both the past and the future as well as the present.

The cross, then, is not merely an event in history, once upon a time. It includes also the spoken word of preaching and the sacraments. Thus in the cross Christ brings us victory over death, evil, and the devil—over death since by saying, "Christ despoils Hades," John means that Christ by his victory has shown that meaning triumphed over meaninglessness; over evil since man's defect (failing to be that for which he was created) is overcome by "opening of the gates of Paradise"; over the devil since the demonic forces are overcome by internal effects.

In summary, this was a cosmic victory because:

(1) The cross happened at a certain time and place in history.

(2) The cross affected all of time, past, present, and future.

(3) The effects of the cross can be seen in the course of history as realized in the hearts and lives of the believers.

(4) The victory of the cross is brought home to us through the ministry of the word and the sacraments.

Another fundamental idea behind the patristic theory is that of sacrifice—giving what is due to God. Obedience and praise are due to God in that Christ gave the perfect sacrifice not to offended deity but as the first-fruit of a restored humanity. In the West one of the most meaningful writers for the patristic view was Athanasius (293-373) in his treatise on *The Incarnation of the Word of God*.

He begins the treatise by raising the pertinent question, "Why is it that the Word of the Father became manifest in human form?" The answer is simply stated that it was for the salvation of man. This brings a lengthy discussion on why man needed to be saved. Salvation can not be explained apart from creation.

According to Athanasius, God made all things out of nothing through his own Word. Man was given a special place because he was bestowed with God's grace—the impress of his own image. It was this grace whereby a man became reasonable and through this reasonableness he, in some limited degree, was able to express the mind of God. Yet, this life of grace was conditional upon the will of man. Thus it could continue forever or be turned away. The conditions imposed by God were a place, paradise, and a law with a single prohibition. If man guarded the grace and retained the loveliness of the original innocence, then the life of paradise would be his forever.

If man went astray, he would no longer live in paradise but continue outside of it in death and corruption. The deepest penalty was not death but corruption. This corruption was a kind of returning to nonbeing. Thus arose a need for redemption. As man had been called out of nonexistence, he was now in danger of returning again to nonexistence. If God did not intervene, this would undo the work of God. If God intervened and man did not die, this would make God out to be a liar. Thus God faced the two horns of a dilemna. What could he do?

If only trespass were involved, repentance would be sufficient. But corruption having set in, it was necessary for the Word of God himself to enter the world in a new way. Since the Word could not die, it was necessary to assume a body capable of death. This meant taking upon himself our body from a spotless, stainless virgin—a pure body. Who was to do the task? Men and angels were both unequal to it. Thus, the coming of the very image himself, our Savior Jesus Christ was the answer. God, being faithful, now sought to renew the image of God in man by himself taking on a human body. Then, surrendering his body to death, Jesus Christ offered it to the

Father for us all. This he did out of sheer love for us so that in his death all might die, and the law of death be abolished. Having fulfilled in his body that for which the law of death was appointed, it was thereafter voided of its power for men.

By this sacrifice Christ was able to rend the veil of man's sin by making an end to the law of death and corruption. But salvation is more than merely forgiveness of sin; the veil of man's ignorance must also be rent. To enter into fellowship with God, knowledge of God is essential—knowledge not only *that* God is but *what* God is. Without this knowledge, existence becomes purposeless. God had created man capable of knowing Him who created him. There were three ways open to knowing God: (1) by looking into the heavens and seeing the harmony of creation; (2) by talking with holy men; and (3) by living the good life through knowing and following the law. In spite of these ways of knowing God, men were rejecting the knowledge of God and becoming brute beasts rather than reasonable men.

Now, since God became man in Christ, there is no excuse for man not knowing *what* God is as well as *that* He is. Man looking for God on the human level could find him ever there. That he was God could be attested by the mighty works he performed.

Why the Word had to die publicly and upon a cross Athanasius now proceeds to explain. When a natural man dies from ordinary causes, it is the result of man's natural weakness. But the Word did not possess the natural weakness of the flesh. Thus the Word must not have seemed to die under ordinary circumstances. Further, to have avoided death would have been to make the resurrection impossible. With no resurrection, there would have been no redemption. Thus, the Word accepted death at the hands of man in order completely to destroy death in his own body. As the supreme object of his coming into the world was to bring salvation to man and as this was impossible without the resurrection of the body before all, it was absolutely essential for the Word first to die.

But why could he not have had an honorable death instead of the ignominy of the cross? If the Word was allowed to choose the kind of death he would die, it would seem as if he could conquer only if he could choose the battleground. This might possibly have given some people ground for disbelieving the resurrection. Having said this, Athanasius goes on to show that there was rich meaning in the cross as the means of death.

First, death on the cross left his body intact giving no excuse for those who would later wish to divide his body, the Church. Second, the Scripture needed to be fulfilled. "Cursed be everyone who hangs on a tree."[1] The Word was to become a curse. Third, dying with his hands outstretched on the cross served as a symbol that he invited both Jew and Gentile to come to him. Finally, his death on a cross allowed him to be lifted off the ground and to purify the very air which had become polluted.

Critics of the patristic view have raised some serious questions directed toward those who hold this theory.

---

[1]Galatians 3:13.

What is the origin and nature of the devil? Could he be trusted to make a bargain with God? Is it possible to have an adequate view of God expressed in extremely legalistic language?

(2) The objective theory was held by Anselm (1033-1109) who interpreted Christ's work as the satisfaction of the honor of God injured by man's sin, as the act of atoning God's judgment and wrath by Christ's vicarious suffering.

The question of why God could not forgive those who could not pay troubled the reformers. They sought to evade the difficulty by declaring that by His very nature God could not forgive man without demanding a penalty that would do justice to the greatness of sin, since it was not only a matter of satisfying God's love, but also his holiness which demanded righteousness. If God forgave sin lightly, he would not be righteous in the highest sense of the word. Hence Christ, God's Son, voluntarily bore the penalty of sinful man that God might freely forgive by his grace and yet be righteous.

Though the question of how God could save by grace and yet be righteous was answered to the satisfaction of some, others asked whether there were two attributes in God which opposed each other. Is there a dualistic strife between love and holiness within God's nature?

This view brought to light a weakness in the concept of God, the Father, and God, the Son. The love of God comes to be associated with Christ and the justice of God with the Father. This results in a serious logical inconsistency—Christ is held to be one with God and yet he differs from him in his fundamental nature. Hence, it would not be true that he that hath seen the Son hath seen the Father. Although the objective view answered some questions raised by the critics of the patristic view, more serious questions arose from the theory.

(3) The subjective theory or moral influence theory is connected first with the name of Peter Abelard (1079-1142) and since Abelard with the Liberal movement. This view interprets the work of Christ as the revelation in word and deed of the forgiving love of God inspiring in us love for God and man. The main stress of this view was the need for man to be changed, not God. The work of Christ, then, consisted in changing man's attitude toward God. Jesus became the supreme example of one who discovered the power of God.

The weakness of this view, according to some of its critics, was the place of God in the atonement. It posed the questions: Did Christ really need to die to save us? Did God do anything special at all that man could not have done for himself? Was not Jesus' sacrifice merely human achievement, in the final analysis? The tendency was to reduce love to sentimentalism. In the subjective theory God's love was more concerned for man's comfort than for man's moral character. It failed to show the depth of God's suffering for a world.

Nels Ferré in criticizing this view says,

But neither can we reduce the doctrine of the Atonement to the limits of the moral influence subjective theory. The feeling in this emphasis is too much that of "salvation by character." . . . This theory, therefore, if taken by itself, is obviously both unrealistic and unchristian, for Christianity is through and through a God-centered religion according to which man without God's redemptive grace is lost in his trespasses and sins.[3]

(4) Gustaf Aulén presents the classic view in his book, *Christus Victor*. This view presents God's forgiveness as God's unconditional, unmotivated way to man, the great mystery of the divine drama which is inaccessible to any and all rational apprehension. It is a divine mystery which takes place contrary to all reason. In this view, Christ's death and descent into hell was for the purpose of paying to the devil a ransom for the redemption of mankind from the power of Satan and hell. In paying ransom to the devil, God was reconciling himself, for the devil is God's agent. This explanation of the atonement limits the work of reconciliation to God.

Through Jesus Christ, God entered into the stream of human history and engaged the forces of evil in decisive combat. These evil forces are cosmically conceived. God defeats the devil, and thereby releases man from the bondage into which his sinful rebellion has brought him. God's nature is love, and the atonement is throughout an act of love. Through it God brings about fellowship between himself and men on the basis of his grace. What God has done historically through Christ's life and death and resurrection he does continually in the act of justifi-

[3]From *The Christian Faith*, pp. 156-157. Copyright 1942 by Harper & Brothers. Used by permission.

cation. The decisive factor is the victory of God's love over all that opposes it.

Since no one theory is adequate, we might do well to state the main points of the atonement as we see it.

(1) God is the subject of the atonement. He is the reconciler as well as the reconciled. There is no way God can be considered as the passive receiver of a sacrifice or satisfaction offered by man or Christ in man's behalf.

(2) Sin and salvation must be conceived in completely personal terms.

(3) Concerning the Incarnation, God is the actual subject. It is God's entrance into humanity to struggle against the tyrants which culminates in his death and resurrection.

Summarizing, we can say that when we speak of God's atonement, we mean that God suffers for man's sin and yearns for the day when that which separates man from God is taken away. This suffering for sin is an *eternal drama* in the nature of God. It is impossible to have a concept of God as love and not admit the fact that God is capable of the deepest suffering, a suffering that is different qualitatively from man's suffering. The cause, or that which leads to God's suffering, is the present separation between God and man. This is the obstacle or sin which the atonement of God is to overcome.

How God overcomes the obstacle of sin and makes it possible for him to effect his purpose of bringing man forward to fellowship with himself and through him with his fellow man can be understood only against the backdrop of the cross of Christ and the life that preceded it.

In the cross we see most clearly God's will to love. The quality of love revealed in the suffering of the cross is different in kind from the quality of love we call human love, which is never without a mixture of selfishness. This kind of love, made real in the life and particularly seen in the death of Christ, we call holy love. In the holy love of God revealed in the cross, God presents his alternative to man's way of life. The very essence of God's love is its concern for others; therefore, by its very nature it is creative of fellowship. It is meeting evil with a kind of love which not only forgives in the sense of human indifferent condoning, but has a vital concern for the best interest of the one forgiven. Thus Nels Ferré writes,

There is tension in God. God's love yearns for fellowship with His children but His holiness, which is the purity and wisdom of His love, demands that it be on the basis of love alone. That is why God suffers. He suffers because He loves us with a holy love and in a dimension unknown to us. That is why Calvary is beyond common suffering.[4]

The person forgiven on this basis finds himself in an entirely new relationship to the one who has forgiven him. Ferré points this out in his stimulating and illuminating book, *Know Your Faith*, in answer to a question he raises.

But how do we get right with God? The answer is simple: God has already paved the way for us. God himself came in Jesus Christ as holy universal Love to fulfill the life of past human history in the life of one historical person; his coming paved the way for the fulfillment of the life of every man.[5]

---

[4]Ibid., pp. 172-173.
[5]From *Know Your Faith*, p. 8. Copyright 1959. Used by permission of Harper & Brothers, publishers.

When we really understand the atonement, we can begin to understand why this kind of world is necessary (to grow persons capable of fellowship), why God suffers (God yearns for fellowship yet cannot have it on any less base than holy love for the sake of the one loved), why man is restless (man's deeper self longs for completion). Thus the doctrine of the atonement rightly understood is at the very heart of understanding God and the world and ourselves. To seek to explain the atonement apart from God as holy love is to have only a partial perspective, and a partial perspective can answer only some of the basic questions while the others still vex the mind.

The meaning of the atonement for each person is the expression of or making tangible this holy love which we have received as a gift of God to our fellow man. We are not merely to behold the drama of the cross but to enter into it. Thus, the atonement becomes real as the one forgiven takes up his cross. The atonement has cosmic, universal significance in that the price paid is beyond our rational comprehension. We simply accept it. In his suffering God revealed his love to us while we were yet sinners. In revealing his love, he revealed also his purpose for creation, which is to bring us into a fellowship for which we were made.

In revealing his purpose for fellowship, God has left us eternally unsatisfied until we are united with him through his kind of love.

Man's greatest need, then, is to accept God's salvation. Through Christ man can be freed from the tyranny of self, insecurity, and fragmented time. Past sins are forgiven. Deliverance can be found from the wrath to come, in that we meet now the God we seek to escape but one day must face.

Through God's salvation man can receive a new self, a new society, a new hope for the life to come. Man can enter into fellowship now with the God who is.

Chapter V

The Christian Faith and
Life Everlasting

The Christian faith is a drama. God started it by his creation of the world. He centered it in Christ. How will it end? He created man in his image. Is there some knowledge of the outcome before God rings down the curtain on human history?

If there is not, it is difficult to say whether we live in a good or a bad world. Neither can we deny a basis for the thought of those who look on life as a horror to be escaped. Nor can we avoid a measure of sympathy for the people who lament the brevity of man's earthly existence as proof of its final meaninglessness. In either case, if there be no continuation, life for man ends either in frustration or meaninglessness.

If this be all, it is difficult, indeed, to regard our earthly experience, with all its depths of evil and capacity for tragedy, as the creation and activity of an all-good, all-wise, and all-powerful God. What we now see of life must be only a part of the larger and better whole; otherwise death holds out no promise that what is endured as hard and unpleasant in this life has any meaning to make up for such experiences in a better life to come and death ends what is best for some people—life itself. But is earthly life merely a part of the whole?

In the light of all of our modern knowledge, can we still believe in life after death? The Christian faith knows only one answer to this question: God who is love cannot abandon the children he has created. Life after death is as real as God in Christ. Life after death is as certain as the centrality of Christ for history. Life after death is as real as truth, as certain as faith, and as dependable as God's love. Neither death nor anything else in creation shall ever be able to separate us from the love of God in Christ. God is not the God of the dead but of the living.

As Paul says: "Who shall separate us from the love of Christ? Shall tribulation, or distress, or persecution, or famine, or nakedness, or peril, or sword? . . . No, in all these things we are more than conquerors." (Romans 8:35, 37.)

We do not believe this because of speculative reasoning or the scientific evidence of a spiritualistic kind, because of the heartbreak of human loneliness or the ache of bereft love. The Christian hope springs neither from sophisticated philosophy nor from primitive psychology. It is the offspring neither of rational fancy nor of emotional frenzy. The central conviction undergirding the Christian witness to everlasting life is belief in the resurrection of Jesus Christ. Here faith enters into pioneer territory all alone, without the help either of reason or of science; for just as reason finds itself puzzled by the testimony, so science remains helpless to reproduce the facts.

Yet the Christian believes. He believes because he has seen the face of deathless love in Jesus Christ; because the community of believers, of which he is now one, stood ready to die for the testimony that Christ was risen; and because such a rising is consistent with the character of the God he knows and sees at work in human history for man's salvation. He believes because the witnesses gave us the miracles of the New Testament and the Church. He believes because a new age of human history started with Jesus Christ; and because the resurrection story has already begun in his own life.

The resurrection of Jesus provides the source of our faith in life after death. When reason becomes creative and critical within the Christian faith, man no longer believes that the God revealed in and through Christ can permit life to end in destruction. God as the sovereign Lord who is saving love, now and forever, cannot fail. Just as God raised Christ, so also shall he raise all men with him.

The Christian faith demands that there is life after death although man must leave the exact description of it to those who have gone before. God has put a limit to our knowledge purposefully. Whenever anyone becomes graphic and specific about life after death, "believe him not and follow him not," says Jesus. God has put a curtain between us and life after death so that while we live here, our attention may be given to our tasks here even though our hope has already rent the veil.

Yet life after death will be subject to God's holy love. God is never sentimental. His love is holy. He permits us to do many things contrary to his will and to continue denying his purposes for a very long time. He gives us more and more rope. He extends the area of our freedom. He lengthens the time of our liberty. Such freedom, however, is completely accountable. God holds us responsible for our full use of it.

We abuse this freedom and sin results. Because God is holy and because his holiness is inviolate, sin must be paid for. Sin involves guilt and consequences. Guilt is a matter of personal relations. Consequences are the way the world works out its righteousness in cause and effect. When a man murders, he is guilty and his crime bears consequences. He sins against persons and initiates a chain of physical consequences beyond personal feelings and acceptance or rejection. The relatives of the murdered man may forgive the murderer, a human court remit his guilt, and a chief of state pardon him. But the dead man stays dead.

Though God forgives our guilt when he restores relationships, he does not stop consequences. Even though in Jesus Christ, God has shown himself ready to declare guiltless by grace anyone who repents, the forgiven have to work to correct the consequences of their deeds and the deeds of others. However completely we may be forgiven, we must assume on the other side of the grave the responsibility of our deeds done in the body. The holiness of God is not only inviolate but eternal.

The ending depends on God and also on us. God's part in the ending is threefold.

(1) The first point is that God created all things for a perfectly good end. God is; he is love eternal, all-wise, and has all the power there is. When God created the world, he knew what he was doing; he was morally responsible; he left no weakness in it; he foresaw the final result; he knew what kind of world was going to result; and he had sufficient means to guide those results to a finally good purpose.

God did give man freedom. Man's freedom is a real and great privilege; it is never forced. Yet freedom is never free except within fulfillment of one's nature. God therefore will not violate man's freedom but he has so made man that he cannot be free in fulfillment until he accepts God's will.

God demonstrated his respect for freedom by so making man that he can never be free until he finds his freedom within the love of God. God made man's freedom so much a part of his true nature that man can never be satisfied until he chooses the freedom of life that can be found only within the life of love.

When God created the world, he gave man no more freedom than he could handle. Sometimes he seems to have too much freedom. He can commit suicide or he can destroy his own civilization. He can commit the most hideous crimes. The familiar story of the ostriches might illustrate this truth. The baby ostrich complains to its mother, "Look at man, he has learned to fly around the world! We had a better start and we can scarcely fly at all." The mother ostrich replied, "Man is flying too fast. Since the world is round, man, one day, will fly so fast that he will hit himself from behind in a tremendous rear-end accident and never know that what hit him was himself." Man seems to have the freedom to destroy himself.

If this life were all, man's freedom would have to be regarded as an irresponsible gift. But God gave man a deep stubborn freedom in order that the final product might be truly in accordance with his greatness as Creator. God also made that freedom to be exercised within immeasurable time. Man has time to go on long detours, to wander at length in the wilderness, to go into foreign countries, to starve, and to be ashamed before he returns home. However, life's fears and hatreds never cease to be intermingled with some kindness and with some touch of love.

God's freedom, furthermore, is more real and stronger than man's. Therefore, God agonizes over man's sin and lostness, he mourns over man's faithlessness and rebellion, and he longs for man's homecoming. Indeed, God cannot be fully free until man returns home. God lets himself be bound in love and leaves man to go his own way until he finds God's way best for him.

(2) The second point is that God knew man would be faithless and rebellious before he created the world. He knew man would have to go his own way in order to become free and mature in love. Sin did not take God by surprise. But, because God created the world responsible,

he also prepared his proper remedy for sin before the foundations of the world. "The Lamb was slain before the foundation of the world. . . ."

From the beginning God put the cross at the center of world history. God knew man would never have the power to save himself. He made man dependent both on himself and others that he might discover the glory of community. God created man in need of God and his fellow men in order that only the divine society could finally fulfill life. God knew that he himself would have to come in the fullness of time to save man. He knew that man could be won only by suffering love. Consequently he purposed eternally to save man through Jesus Christ.

He determined to come in his fullness, Christ-love, and in the fullness of time to fill a man full with himself. This purpose was part of creation; the particular man, Jesus Christ, was part of human history. Universal holy love entered Jesus as the Christ that through a new being man might be made Man. God's freedom to save became free through man's freedom to find. The Son of God became Son of man that through him all men might enter the kingdom of heaven.

God planned the cross for man's salvation before he created man. God knew that man could not find salvation except as he himself entered fully into man's sinful situation and from within gave him the power to overcome sin. God foresaw that the healing medicine of eternal life could be only God's life given freely in suffering for man. But it also involved man's life given freely in suffering back to God and through the power of God for man.

Such is the meaning of the cross, the center of human history long before human history ever started.

The centrality of the cross requires the community of the cross. God provided such community in the cross. We call this community the Church. Only at the cross do we learn for ourselves what it means to have no motivation beside Jesus Christ and him crucified. Only at the cross is there a true door to heaven, a door of experience that leads into heaven by the way of an open tomb.

Those who have entered by the door have to become witnesses. The mouth speaks from the fullness of the heart. Those whose mouths make no confession of Christ as Lord know not the God of love within. The Christian faith is by nature a witnessing faith. Evangelism as a natural witness to God's love in Christ is as inevitable as the Christian faith itself. Missions as the outreach of the glorious gospel "of Jesus and his love" is as necessary as the Christian experience of Christ. The story is told concerning one of America's great Negro singers. He was singing the spiritual, "I'm a Witness for my Lord." After he had sung a number of stanzas, including: "Moses was a witness, a witness for my Lord," "Daniel was a witness, a witness for my Lord," his grey-haired mother sitting near the front, rose to her feet and sang, "Hallelujah, I'm a witness, a witness for my Lord." This experience is universal in the heart of the believer.

To belong to Christ is to have God for Father, Jesus for elder Brother and all men for family. No family joy and peace can be experienced fully until the family of God is complete. The attention in the Christian family is, of course, not on joy and peace as selfish cravings but on those members of the family who lack these joys. True joy and peace crave to be shared. God provided the need for the community of the cross and the overflowing Christian witness as part of the sufficient means of salvation he ordained for man before he made the world.

(3) The third point stems from the fact that God's love never runs out. God is love eternally. His love is so different from our love that we cannot really fathom its deepest meaning. Even though God has revealed himself in Jesus Christ, he is far beyond our full understanding.

God is not hampered by our limits of time. His time is eternal. Eternity means more than mere duration. Eternity means that God creates time. He is the Lord of his own time. For God, time never can come to an end. Therefore no man should dare set a limit to the time of God. Limitless time is always at the service of God's faithful love.

God, moreover, has all the resources necessary for man's salvation. He has the resources that enabled him not to create man irresponsibly. God commanded the means to create man with a freedom that was real, without denying his own freedom. God never surrenders his control over man's freedom. God made man capable of being changed.

Our salvation, however, does not depend on God alone. It depends also on us. God has given us a real measure of freedom that he will never violate. As long as we refuse to accept him, we hurt him, we injure ourselves, and we help spoil the world he has made.

As far as man is concerned, the ending is clear—it depends on us individually.

The ending can never be fulfilled until each one of us makes a decision in freedom. We have freedom guaranteed by God himself. To be sure, our freedom is of two kinds: freedom of choice and freedom of life. The more important freedom is freedom of life. We can have freedom of choice without freedom of life, but we can never have freedom of life without freedom of choice. We can keep freedom of choice and forfeit freedom of life.

As long as we remain apart from God, we choose freedom of choice for unfreedom of life. We choose to have our own way even when it goes against God's way. We choose darkness rather than light. We begin to feel that we can eternally defy God. We think that we can be as free as God; we think that we can be as big as God. Thus we repeat the original sin. Original sin is best expressed as the camouflaged conviction that God made man free for choice, not for life.

The nature of the ending depends on us. We must choose it. We are free but we also have reason. We can realize that we are not free in the sense of fulfillment so long as we use our freedom for slavery to self. We can see that frustration is not freedom of life even though we are free to choose it. We can know that fulfillment of our whole and true self is freedom both of choice and of life.

We can preserve and fulfill our own freedom only by choosing God's way. Only in God's service freely chosen can we enjoy perfect freedom both of choice and of life. God gave us devotion to freedom that devotion to the choice of freedom might at length lead us to the free choice of the free life.

God not only gave us freedom to choose the greater freedom; he gives us frustration when we reject fulfillment. Freedom wrongly used leads to hell; freedom rightly used leads to heaven. Freedom wronged leads to distortion and destruction of life; freedom accepted in God's way leads to harmony and enhancement of life.

Hell is the outworking of the consequences of sin. Hell is freely chosen but not freely endured. Hell catches up with the sinner. Although hell may begin in this life as a foretaste, hell here is only a beachhead. For our sake God makes us face the consequences of what we have done. Hell is guilt and consequences coming together after death. Hell is a place as well as a condition. It is *where* people are as well as *how* they are.

God gave us freedom and reason. If we are wise, we choose the freedom of life now. If we are unwise, we choose hell now. No matter what our choice, we cannot escape God's love. God's love never fails and never ends. If we make our bed in hell, we will find that God is there —as the Judge who frustrates our freedom and speaks to our fear.

Fear has torments. Love casts out fear and fulfills reason. Hell is as real, as just, as disciplinary as God's good will for us. By choosing our own will rather than God's, moreover, we help to increase the world's sin, sorrow, and pain. We prolong the world's agony. We cheat both God and the world.

When we choose God, however, we choose to help others and ourselves. With Paul we do all for the sake of the gospel that we may share in its blessings. Our choice, however, matters most to God. Our choice of his will pleases him whom no tongue can ever begin to describe. He cares as we can never care. Our choice of God's will in Christ, of love, of the cross and the crown, makes the heavenly hosts rejoice. Our choice of salvation will make our own heart sing. Our choice of the new life in Christ will unify our whole self and give us grace and glory.

Our choice of God, however, will matter not only to God and self but to others also. Our life will help countless other people to find the way to salvation. Our faith will be breathed into their lives until they begin to breathe with us the heavenly spirit. Our love will warm and thaw out those who are hardened and hurt. Our witness will lead others to the Christ and keep them from hell.

We will also shorten the time of the world's anguish and hasten the appearance of God's great reign. All of us belong together in this new creation. We postpone the coming of God's great climax of creation. We stand in the way of—and even push back!—the glorious comsummation of Christ. We are likewise guilty of immaturity and folly. When we have tried to gather for ourself the world's riches, and not God's, God will say as he did to the rich man who tore down his barns to build larger ones, not "you wicked creature," but "you fool."

What this means ear cannot now hear nor eye now see. We can be sure, however, that God's great glory, when he shall be everything for everyone, will outstrip our most vivid imagination.

What is the ending? It depends on God. But it also depends on us. What will it be for us? Our choice is necessary and matters to God and to all his creatures. For man stands continually before the threshold of some new tomorrow. Each age wonders what the immediate future holds in store for its children. Thus our age looks anxiously and with mixed emotions for the breaking of the new day.

Some time ago I listened to a lecturer in the Midwest describe what he thought might be ahead for America. He talked in glowing words of life relatively free from disease and life expectancy in terms of 200 years. He plotted for us space travel to the moon and distant places. The possibility was mentioned of traveling in space by stepping on the right air path, similar to the olden days of stepping onto a street car. America's food would, then, be grown in the ocean. The Midwest, where the food is now raised, might be turned into an extensive resort area. The home of tomorrow would be constructed with invisible walls that could be rolled back, like today's convertible car, when the weather allowed. It sounded like a thrilling and interesting world, indeed.

While contemplating on what he had portrayed, the scene before me changed and another picture of tomorrow came into my view. Almost 6,000,000 Americans are now reported to be alcoholics with their numbers increasing daily. According to these figures, one out of every 30 persons in the United States is an alcoholic. The casual regard and breakdown of the marriage vow continues at an alarming pace. The adult and juvenile delinquencies have shown no sign of slackening. The increasing mental collapse threatens to become the major health problem of our day. Considering the picture made from these facts, the outlook

is far from thrilling. As one wag remarked, "If the man
of tomorrow lives to be 200 years old, he will be either
drunk or crazy."

Tomorrow and beyond all tomorrows can be the most
glorious future man has ever encountered—

"What no eye has seen, nor ear heard,
nor the heart of man conceived." 1 Corinthians 2:9.

Or tomorrow and beyond all tomorrows can be the most
devastating era man has ever known—far worse than man
can now conceive.

In Luke 21:28 Jesus says to his disciples, "When these
things begin to take place, look up and raise your heads,
because your redemption is drawing near." Can we in
our day rediscover this hope?

The answer will be Yes, if we will commit ourselves to a
living, vital faith that prepares us for the dawn. For Christianity, at its very heart, is the gospel of the resurrection.

For Further Reading

The Layman Reads His Bible   by Jack Suggs

The Layman Learns to Pray   by Lloyd V. Channels

The Layman Builds a Christian Home   by Vera Channels

Know Your Faith   by Nels F. S. Ferré

Basic Christian Beliefs   by W. Burnet Easton

The Meaning of Christ   by Robert Johnson

And the Life Everlasting   by John Baillie

Life, Death, and Destiny   by Roger Shinn

Date Due